The

MW01518420

Crystal Salt

Origin, active principles and treatments

by

Dr. Jürgen Weihofen

The Essence of the Primeval Sea
Himalayan Crystal Salt

Origin, active principles and treatments
by
Dr. Jürgen Weihofen

Original Edition

sanoform-Verlag GmbH
Ginsterweg 1
51427 Bergisch Gladbach
Germany
phone: +49-2204-22900
fax: +49-2204-64952
e-mail: info@sanoform.de
www.sanoform.de

1st English edition published in 2005
Dr. Jürgen Weihofen
The Essence of the Primeval Sea
Himalayan Crystal Salt -
origin, active principles and treatments

Original title: Essenz des Urmeeres
Himalaya-Kristallsalz -
Herkunft, Wirkprinzipien und Heilanwendungen
Translation by: Dirke Hentschel
Distributed by: www.heartfeltliving.com

Contents

Preface

Our health care system is reaching its limits, both in an economic sense and with regard to its capacity. The era of feasibility mania when people thought all kinds of diseases could be defeated in a scientific approach is now being followed by disillusionment. Today's physicians have succeeded in eradicating disastrous epidemics by means of antibiotics, they are able to re-animate the clinically dead and even transplant human hearts. But when it comes to the ever-increasing number of cancer diseases, allergies, the vast number of chronic illnesses and even trivial colds, they appear to be powerless.

Gradually, a return to traditional well-tried therapies is taking hold, which were brushed off as "old-fashioned" and "obsolete" during the 1950's when many countries saw an economic boom. During initial enthusiasm for defeating diseases with rational reasoning people lost sight of two very essential aspects: man is a live creature, no machine, and man has a soul.

Traditional therapies of the East have preserved the knowledge that man is a creature of body, soul and spirit, and that disease can spring from any of these levels and moreover ought to be treated on all levels. Asian medical science, especially Traditional Chinese Medicine (TCM) and Indian Ayurveda enjoy increasing popularity among patients and therapists, conveying a sense of perceiving and understanding every being as a whole.

But we don't have to stray as far away as that. Up until the 19th century, our traditional nature-oriented medicine also treated man as a whole. The very best example is homeopathy.

No matter which medical approach we look at, we will always find that, apart from medical plants and a health-conscious diet, simple treatments applying heat, cold, water, and salt have significant influence on therapies. Treatments in many spas are based on the stimulus of climate, spa water, seawater or sole (brine). They give vitality and energy and help patients to rediscover their individual balance, thus their own health.

Salt from the Himalayas is more than just an extraordinary food. It dates back to a time without any man-made environmental pollution. It is more pristine than any other food can be today. It stores information from the primeval sea where all existence originates. Crystal salt bears the knowledge of the ideal environment in which all creatures thrive. It helps our body cells return to a wholesome and energetic primitive state.

From ancient times, salt has been an extraordinary and renowned healer. There is no life without salt. I invite you to take an unprejudiced look at the potential of Himalayan crystal salt. I apologise for any possible errors, and I am looking forward to receiving your comments and letters about your personal success with crystal salt.

Bergisch Gladbach, April 2005

Dr. Jürgen Weihofen

About the author:
Dr. Jürgen Weihofen holds an advanced degree in oecotrophology (nutritional science and home economics), and is lecturer and author in the field of health and nutrition.

The Primeval Sea — Origin of all Life

When seeking a holiday to regenerate and re-charge the batteries, when you want to regain some of that old vitality for everyday life, many of us see no alternative but the seaside. In some magical way people have always been drawn to the ocean. In Germany it has become a dictum to say that one is "ripe for the island", meaning he needs a break to get away from it all. To be surrounded by the ocean is an old dream of humanity, which an increasing number of people can fulfil for themselves thanks to today's commercialised tourism.

Yet it is this tourism with its bally-ho and high-rise buildings that has led many stretches of coast to become more similar to big cities. But even here the power and fascination of the sea can be sensed. It draws people to the beach and lets them gaze at the horizon wishfully, as though they sensed that the answer to all of life's questions could be found here.

Old health resorts and spas at the seaside give evidence of more than 200 years of medical treatments taking advantage of the healing effect of the sea, not only improving the immune system but also treating many conditions, chronic diseases of the skin and respiratory system as well as allergies. A prolonged stay at the seaside in one of the numerous salt-based spas, or the visit to a salt grotto often entail a change for the better and not rarely lead to ultimate and permanent recovery.

This effect is enhanced by sun, wind and the mild stimulating climate. Still, the most important aspect for treatment is seawater itself and the salty air. Today's modern version of treatment known as Thalasso therapy is based on traditional knowledge and effectively builds on all of these factors. How come that seawater is good for us? We are not fish but creatures living on the shore. Could it be that there is a profound relationship which most of us are no longer aware of?

Let us trace back the evolution of life and go back to the beginning of the relationship between ocean and man. Historically seen it was Darwin who discovered that mankind is at the end of an uninterrupted evolutionary chain. We are creatures that have gone from strength to strength according to a secret plan of Life, adapting to our environment and developing by differing from our ancestors. Genesis of every single human being reflects this development and makes it comprehensible. From fertilisation to birth, every embryo goes through all stages that evolution went through millions of years ago, only in a condensed way. We spend nine months in salty amniotic fluid before we are born! It is only then that we make the abrupt step to being a breathing creature.

Modern science has proven what the bible has been telling us all along: all life comes from water, from the primeval sea to be more precise. 70% of our planet is covered by oceans to this day; dry land is rather hard to find. In theory, the oceans are big and deep enough for all land to vanish in them. Their greatest depths of more than 11,000 metres are deeper than the height of the highest mountains on shore.

Seawater contains almost the full range of elements and substances. It is the nutrient solution with an abundance of substances from which life was able to emerge four billion years ago. The first giant molecules acquired the ability to reduplicate, i.e. to increase in number, bringing forth the origin of the first micro creatures in the primeval sea. At a later stage, photosynthesis developed, i. e. it became possible for primeval creatures to derive energy directly from sunlight. Seaweed came into existence. Today it is widely accepted that blue algae were the first plants on Earth.

The entire scope of animal life is based on plant life in the ocean. Plankton from algae serves as food for the smallest creatures of the sea. Small crustaceans, krill and molluscs are food for small fish which are in turn food for bigger fish, and so on. Interestingly, only the biggest animals of the sea, the whalebone whale and the whale shark, feed on plankton, too.

It is a well-known fact that the first plants on shore as well as ferns and horsetail rushes bear a close affinity to seaweed. Life came from the ocean and conquered the land. Animals followed into this habitat and adapted to their environment.

It lies in our nature that anything concerned with life on-shore appears to us as being par-

ticularly meaningful. Yet, the land is much less active in a biological sense than the ocean. Little or no life exists in vast areas of deserts and mountains. Life on-shore exists only a few metres below and above ground, whereas life in the ocean has expanded into great depths, has indeed almost fully penetrated its entire volume. An estimated 80% of all biological activity on our planet is located in the sea. Also, the variety of life forms in the ocean is greater than that on-shore. There are endless correlations between them, between shallow and deep areas, between zones low and rich in nutrients, between warm and cold regions of the ocean. We are only slowly recognising the importance of the oceans for our Earth's climate and environment, and we are only beginning to get a glimpse of the massive threats to Earth which are put into effect by human civilisation and which may eventually strike back on us. One aspect of the rising oceans is that our glaciers and poles are melting due to constant global warming. Our climates are heavily impacted because of the mass size of our oceans. They have a moderating effect on temperature fluctuations, have significant relevance on the hydrological cycle, and steer winds and clouds. There is an enormous exchange of oxygen and carbon dioxide in the air. Without the oceans life as it is today would not be possible. And without the primeval sea there would be no life at all.

Anyway, why is seawater salty? Seawater has an average salt content of 3.5%. While the main ingredient of seawater is sodium chloride it also contains all water-soluble minerals. Their sources are rock-forming minerals of the Earth's crust, which are eventually dissolved by rain-water and finally flow into the sea. On average, rivers transport 0.1g of salt per litre towards the ocean. While seawater evaporates, the salt is left behind, and its content has been accumulating there over millions of years. In addition, submarine volcanic eruptions as well as atmospheric substances carried along by the wind add their share to the salt content of the oceans.

Just like the Earth, our human bodies consist of water at a level of 70%. We need dissolved minerals and trace elements because our body cells only thrive in an environment that is equivalent to that of the ocean. Cell pressure is maintained by potassium. To be effective it needs its natural counterpart sodium that is effective outside these cells and without which the entire system would break down. It is a well-known fact that a loss of water cannot be balanced by merely adding pure H_2O; it is vital to also add salt at the same time. We frequently encounter the term "isotonic" which is used for drinks that contain minerals in the same composition as can be found in our blood. Loss of blood can only be balanced by adding saline solution. Considering this fact it becomes clear that even for us humans living on-shore a special relationship with seawater exists. It is our home, the Mother of Life.

White Gold throughout the times

Prehistoric times

In ancient times, man and beast knew instinctively that salt was an essential nutrient for them. Herbivores satisfied their demand of salt by feeding on plants with rich mineral content while carnivores had plentiful supply through their prey. Salt as a nourishment is equally essential for us as water. Yet today, our instinctive desire for salt is more than satisfied by the often immoderate seasoning of food, especially in modern convenience food. Simple cooking salt is at hand everywhere, cheap, and never missing in a savoury dish.

In earlier times, things were different. Only those who lived close to the sea were without concerns about their salt supplies. Consumption of fish and other seafood adequately supplied them with salt. Salt can be extracted by drying up seawater, or small amounts of seawater can be drunk, just as used to be done by the seamen. And even nowadays you will find that in seaside resorts drinking cures involving seawater are common.

It was a tedious and dangerous job to transport the salt that had been extracted from the sea to the heart of the country. Salt is heavy and very sensitive to humidity. It had to be protected from air moisture and rain. Consequently, salt was precious to people living inland and much more expensive than today. To this day, the long trade routes of the merchants are called "salt trails".

Sometimes people were lucky to find their own salt deposits in form of sole (or brine) springs, whereby knowledge of these was treated as a big secret because salt was of utmost economic value to them. To own a sole spring meant to have a secure income. Yes, salt was indeed equivalent to money. Roman soldiers were partially paid in salt; the English term "salary", literally meaning salt money, still gives evidence of this scheme.

Salt made merchants and cities prosper, it was a popular object of trade and of power. It used to rule life in such a way that down to the present day you find traces of it in many names of German and Austrian cities: Salzburg, Salzgitter,

Bad Salzuflen, also Schwäbisch Hall, Halle or Bad Reichenhall, because the Indo-Germanic term for salt was „Hal". Major interconnecting tracks which later turned into country roads still carry names such as "Hellweg" which simply means salt road.

The term "salt" is derived from the Latin word „sal" which is deflected from "sol". A water and salt solution is called "Sole" [so-lay] which can also be translated with "sun". Salt cannot be extracted from seawater without the sun. Crystallisation of salt is enabled through the sun's energy, which prompts the evaporation of water. Salt always contains the sun's energy.

Besides the meaning of salt, the Indo-Germanic term „Hal" – or its deflections „Haal" or „Hall" – also means "vibration" or "sound". Germans know the term "Nachhall" which means an echo, involving vibration. To the Celts "Hal" also meant "health" and "holy", making it clear that our ancestors looked upon salt as more than just a dead mineral. Vibration is pure information beyond the substantial. It hints at some secret knowledge of ancient times, which got lost and has to be re-discovered. It corresponds with insights about regulation processes in our body-spirit-soul entity which e. g. homeopathy makes use of: the most efficient medicine is the one that, from a chemical point of view, contains no more substances but only information; its agent is always water. It can carry information in the weakest dilution, i.e. the highest potency. Salt is always extracted from water and can be re-dissolved in it. Salt extracted from our oceans today unfortunately also contains all information about wastewater and other encumbrances. Salt from the primeval sea, however, which has been stored deep down underneath the Earth for 250 million years is free from such resonation and strikes a yearning chord in us as we long for health and wholesomeness.

At the onset of civilisation there were but few options of preserving food, one of them being the salting. Especially meat and fish were salted and thus preserved as food supply. It was discovered that salt extracts water from organic substances, killing micro organisms which would otherwise greedily lunge at dead protein. Meat and fish, preserved in salt casks, could be stored throughout the winter, which became a vital procedure for seamen. Even vegetables were preserved with salt. Today we still eat pickled cabbage, in Germany known as "Sauerkraut", but in earlier times people also preserved cucumbers, beans, onions, or other vegetable for winter time by storing it between layers of salt or in a saline solution. Meat that is preserved by means of salting, known as cured or pickled meat, is still common today.

Salt in Antiquity

The first tradition of the healing effect of salt dates back to the famous builder and physician Imothep who lived in Egypt during the third century B. C. It is a description of the drying effect that salt has on wounds, thus preventing inflammations.

Salt in Antiquity enjoyed such a high esteem that it was regarded as a holy element or a gift of the Gods. The Old Testament reports that the union between God and his chosen people was sealed by "Jahwe's salt". Salt is another important aspect in the Sermon on the Mount, the central message of the New Testament, as a symbol for an element that nourishes life and brings light and salvation: "You are the salt of the earth, but if salt becomes tasteless, with what will one salt?" Down to this day, salt is used in the Christening rite.

When Alexander the Great between 356 and 323 B. C. advanced the Indian subcontinent across Near India he discovered the deposits of the reddish crystal salt of the Himalayas. This salt was so valuable that people started to mine it and – enduring unthinkable exertions – transport it by elephants across the Hindukush mountains to Europe. Under the name of "Emperor's salt" this valuable salt was exclusively reserved for the Emperor's family.

In Antiquity salt was not merely a vital food but also a remedy. Dioskurides, a famous physician to Roman Emperors, describes it as follows: "Salt belongs to every meal. He, who uses it with common sense, will have a long life, enjoy it happily, for his own good, for the sake of re-production in his family, and for the good of the community, for salt is life itself." He recommended salt as a laxative and warm seawater packs for skin diseases. As early as then he recommended rock salt as the strongest of all.

Salt in the Middle Ages

Salt played an important role in medieval customs and conventions at table. Hospitality was demonstrated by sharing bread and salt with guests. Salt was presented in precious jars, which were placed on the table according to the standing and the rank order of the guests. It was cut off a big chunk and then crushed. But it was not until the 19th century that the white, free-flowing, fine salt became available. The old salt kegs were replaced by shakers with punched lids from which the salt could be sprinkled directly onto the dishes.

In so-called sole springs the precious raw material was brought to the surface by a natural process. Mining was initially done by manual scooping. In Germany's Bad Reichenhall mechanic scooping works with revolving chains, known as "paternoster scoops", were introduced in the 14th century, facilitating the scooping of sole from a well shaft. The salt content was at an average of 21.3% (25.6% being the maximum salt content of saturated sole or brine). In boiling houses salt was yielded by evaporating sole using large pans. In a second step the moisture had to be removed from the salt in drying houses. Sole with less salt content was concentrated by way of the so-called grading technique which allowed the manufacturers to save fuel: the sole trickled down layers of straw from a scaffold, and then down layers of black-thorn. In many health resorts these grading works are still in use today for therapeutic bene-fits: they enhance the salt content of the air, al-leviating respiratory disorders.

1611 saw the outbreak of a „salt war" between the Duchy of Bavaria and the archbishopric of Salzburg. Only in 1829 could the war over salt finally be settled in a "saline contract".

In the 16th century the famous physician Paracelsus was of the opinion that only salted food could be digested properly. He recom-mended salt for the treatment of wounds and sole baths for skin diseases.

In Paracelsus' days, healing skills and alchemy were not controversial. In his view of the world, which saw the microcosm and the macrocosm in relation to one another, he elevated salt to the rank of a basic element. According to his theory, salt stood in between the other two secondary elements sulphur and mercury, combining the principle of combustibility (sulphur is highly inflammable) with the principle of liquidity and volatility (mercury is liquid, evaporates and condenses again). Salt itself reflected permanence, solidity (= the Earth), in other words ashes or minerals. In a way he was quite right with his theory, considering the fact that today salt is the basic substance for major parts of the chemical industry.

Formation of rock salt deposits

The majority of rock salt deposits were formed 250 to 230 million years ago. In the Permian era the Earth's continents did not exist the way they are today, but the total land was fused into a super continent known as Pangea. Europe lay further south by 30 to 40 degrees of latitude and near the equator, India even further south. In the course of Earth's history continents arose and oceans dried up. Shallow seas and lagoons, cut off from the primeval sea by the rising of land, saw solar evaporation in a hot, desert-like dry climate. Such sedimentation tanks were virtually sealed off by a barrier, preventing saturated sole (or brine) from draining off and fresh seawater from infiltrating. Since the various salt minerals each have a different solubility in water they settle at different times. Gypsum is hard to solubilise and is therefore the first to sediment, calcium sulfate follows and finally, when the major part of seawater has evaporated, sodium chloride. The crystallising salt from seawater remained in the shape of small grains. These salt sediments grew to substantial layers and were covered by dust and soil in the course of geological changes.

Eventually Pangea fell apart; the single continents, thus divided, began to drift into different directions on semi fluid crusty plates. In some places they pressed against each other and caused mountains to fold up. In the process of these movements some salt sediments were shifted far below the Earth's surface, where they were subject to immense pressure and thus compressed.

What is salt?

Salts are compounds of smallest, negatively and positively charged particles, known as ions. Common salt consists of positively charged sodium ions and negatively charged chlorine ions, forming a cubic space lattice. The intertwined lattices consisting of sodium and chlorine ions are shifted into two directions by half the edge length of a unit cell. Common cubic lattice models are highly idealised because in reality the electronic clouds of the positive sodium and the negative chlorine ions touch one another. Each ion is surrounded by six ions of the other type in octahedral form. Modern techniques enabled the identification of the edge length of one unit cell. One cubic centimetre of crystal salt contains 1.8×10^{22} unit cells (a figure with 22 zeros).

The chemical term is sodium chloride, the formula NaCl. But there are more types of salt than just common salt. Further salt minerals are e.g. sulfates such as gypsum, or carbonates such as lime. The mineral is internationally called "halite". Salt crystals are of cubic shape and colourless in their pure form. The addition of other substances can cause different tints: reddish, yellowish and brownish colours are caused by tiny inclusions of ferric oxide, e.g. hematite or limonite. In exceptional cases crystals were known to have an edge length of up to one metre. When cleaving rock salt, the cutting edge of the crystals is always perfectly parallel to their cubic face; you will always get rectangular cubes or rectangular cuboids. The smaller the chopped off crystals, the less can be seen of their original tint. Instead of shining through, the light is refracted at the edges, thus the crystals appear to be of white colour.

Mining of salt

Yielding salt from seawater

The probably oldest method of mining salt is the drying up of seawater. It mimics natural processes that take place under favourable terms and account for the largest deposits bearing salt from the primeval sea. Today approx. 50 million tons of sea salt are yielded through systematic commercial salt mining in saline works.

For the purpose of evaporation at least three shallow basins are arranged successively on lowland shores, each one connected to the other by a sealable outlet. Seawater is infiltrated into the first basin. The salt content increases through evaporation. The sole is channelled into the next basin, which is slightly smaller, thus concentrating the salt content in several steps. In the final basin the salt crystallises and can then be gathered into large heaps.

The process of concentrating the sole in several steps and the mechanic gathering of crystallising salt almost exclusively renders sodium chloride as a result, while remaining types of salt and other elements are largely eliminated.

Mining of salt from sole springs, through wet mining and deep drill mining

Natural spring water is salty when it has taken its course through bedrock bearing salt before it comes to daylight. In earlier times people used this salty spring water – also known as spring sole – to yield salt by boiling the water. During the 16th century people tried to procure salt water by drilling well holes in specific places. Even earlier than that, they infiltrated fresh water into mountains in so-called wet mines. The fresh water dissolved the salt, was piped back from deep layers and forwarded to the saline down in the valley.

Today, saturated sole is mined in deep drill mining processes by means of a double-walled pipe system. Fresh water is pumped into the salt deposit through the outside pipe while the water pressure in the inside pipe causes the saturated sole to rise up.

All these three mining procedures have in common the fact that the crystalline salt is initially dissolved in water and later re-crystallised in form of pure evaporated salt. Even in Medieval times it was known that boiling sole in pans also effects a separation process. The sole was left to settle in the pan, from which the workers shovelled the salt crystals. All impurities as well as magnesium and calcium salts which caused a yellowish tinge and gave it a bitter taste were concentrated in the sole and could thus be separated.

Dry mining of rock salt

Rock salt sediments stemming from the primeval sea are sometimes deposited deep down underneath the Earth's surface. In favourable places, however, there are salt outcrops and the mining of these has demonstrably been going on since prehistoric times. We have proof of systematic mining by pitmen since approx. 1,000 B. C. While the men initially worked with their own hands, mechanic devices were eventually used increasingly as the mining of salt proceeded into greater depths. Today, virtually every mine takes advantage of drilling and blasting methods and uses excavators and trucks to remove the salt. There are only few salt mines on Earth in which the salt is cleaved without the aid of technical devices, e.g. in the Pakistani salt deposits of the Himalayas. However, narrations relating to the cleaving of salt "manually" or "by hand" should not be taken too seriously. Of course, people cannot mine rock salt without the use of tools. If no large tools and blasting techniques are to be used, the only method of mining crystal salt gently in a way that is feasible and can be guaranteed is by using small hand tools. The most important aspect is to produce intact crystals that are as big as possible and to make sure they are not dissolved and re-crystallised to pure evaporated salt, which is unfortunately the case with industrial salt production. Refined evaporated salt consists of 99.9% sodium chloride, i.e. it is deprived of all collateral minerals as well as all information contained therein.

Processing of salt

There are a number of unprocessed, unrefined sea salts available. However, the way they are produced qualifies them as common salts only. Salt mined in salt works can never contain the entire range of all substances that are found in seawater.

Salt from salt mines is usually dissolved in water and then produced and refined in the same way as salt derived from sole or from deep drill mining. Today sole is no longer evaporated in large open pans but fully automatically in a continuous process in closed evaporator containers. Spin-off salts are removed beforehand by adding lime and soda. This production process yields common salt consisting of 99.95% to 99.99% pure sodium chloride. Process steam is used to bring the sole to a boil, the salt mash that has settled down is drained in centrifuges and dried with hot air. According to the demands of chemical and food industries and for home cooking, various types of salt are produced by compacting the salt and by adding anti-caking and free-flowing agents. For the sake of easy sprinkling from saltshakers, salt grains are normally coated with sodium carbonates (E 500), silicium oxide (E 551), or sodium ferrocyanide (E 535).

While in Medieval times approx. 150 saline or salt mines existed all over Europe, of which only few were able to produce a few hundred pounds of salt per year, Europe's salt production today is concentrated on just a few big plants, all of which produce several hundreds of thousands of tons of salt every year. Some production plants produce more than one hundred different types of salt, all differing in granularity and composition.

Granularity of common cooking salt should range from 0.2 to 0.8 mm. The even finer powder salt with a granularity of less than 0.1 mm is used in the production of sausages and cheese. Salt for pickling meat and sausages has an added 0.5% to 0.6% sodium nitrite. Salt with larger granularity, which is produced in steaming pans, is used for pretzel-style or lye rolls and in salt mills.

Salt taxes dating from royal salt monopolies survived the centuries until modern times.

Therefore, salt that was not destined for human diet had to be denatured by adding e.g. ferrous oxide. Salt for livestock and road salt was thus rendered inedible and could then be traded without the burden of salt taxes.

Those who value a literally primary salt, which contains all collateral minerals and bears crystal structures that have not changed in 250 million years, for their own nutrition and for remedy purposes will certainly refrain from buying refined salt from saline. Pure crystal salt cleaved from salt mines ought to be preferred, not dissolved and re-crystallised but original, available in chunks or slightly granulated. When used for seasoning this salt is ground in a salt mill shortly before use. Such a crystal salt adds a special taste to dishes, which goes beyond the mere "salty" sensation. Refined salt is out of the question anyway for any therapeutic application, be it externally or internally. Since you want to have the "sea effect" in your treatment you will want to use a salt which provides as many substances as possible that are found dissolved in seawater. Those who are convinced that nature provides the best of whatever we need will certainly also have strong opinions on artificially iodised and fluoridated salt, rendering a discussion about this topic superfluous here.

The importance of salt for our body

Saline solutions are a good example of how important salt is for the human organism. The Scottish physician William B. O´Shaughnessey was the first to balance the loss of salt and fluids in Cholera patients, caused by diarrhoea, with an intravenous saline solution. In 1832 this method was successfully applied for the first time.

Today it is used in modern medicine as the standard infusion solution with a salt content of 0.9%, which corresponds exactly to the fluid properties of blood plasma. In first aid, isotonic saline solution is often crucial for saving life when a great loss of blood is involved. It is the carrier substance for most medical infusions and can also be used for subcutaneous or intramuscular injection. Due to its analogy to body fluids and its tolerability it is highly suitable for clysters and irrigations, e.g. when applying catheters to the gastrointestinal tract and the bladder. Nasal douches, too, are carried out exclusively with saline solutions.

Why is it that an isotonic solution has a different effect on body cells than pure water? The answer lies in the functionality of the outer cell layer, i.e. the cell membrane. It has two essential functions: warding off external influences on one hand and exchanging substances on the other. Nutrients and energy arrive at body cells through the membrane, and decomposed substances of the cell metabolism are excreted by it, too. For this purpose the membrane is partially porous to water and dissolved substances. It is also called semi-permeable membrane. It maintains a certain level of pressure inside the cell by binding water to dissolved substances.

In case of there being a gradient in different degrees of solution a balancing tendency exists: dissolved substances move to a region of lower concentration while water moves to a region of higher concentration. A cell that is surrounded by pure water is therefore exposed to a potential loss of its substances. It is only with high input of energy that the cell can fend this off for some time, but eventually it collapses, leading to cell death. If, however, the solution concentration inside these cells is the same as outside there is no such threat. A higher saline concentration outside the cell is equally detrimental: it would draw water from within the cell causing the cell to dry up. The isotonic, i.e. ideal solution concentration for osmosis, is neutral and does not cause problems to cell metabolism or cell pressure.

This is reflected directly by the correct level of salt intake for human organisms. Insufficient salt intake causes a decrease in blood pressure as well as other disorders. Human bodies require at least 5 to 6 grams of sodium chloride per day to balance losses. The kidneys of most people can regulate excessive salt consumption as long as they are provided with a sufficient level of water. But even excessive consumption of water can cause the regulation process to fail, causing again serious disorders. Consequently, people can die from an overdose of salt as well as from an insufficient intake of salt. Common salt – generally believed to be quite harmless – can actually kill someone. It only depends on the quantum. This clearly underscores Paracelsus' insight that the dosage alone decides about whether or not a substance is poisonous.

To always find the appropriate measure is considered an art, not only in nutrition. This is true for single foods: living on a varied diet and moderating the consumption of favourite dishes and drinks is a simple rule for a healthier life, though not always feasible in practice. The same rule is also true for the ingredients in our food. For many substances we know how much our body needs of them and where the margins lie – upper and lower - at which they become unhealthy for us.

Common salt or sodium chloride is a mineral indispensable to life, which our organism needs essentially to perform and maintain bodily functions. Sodium chloride dissolves and dissociates in water, i.e. in our body fluids, into the charged particles $Na+$ and $Cl-$, also called ions or electrolytes. In blood plasma, lymph and intra cellular as well as extra cellular space these are the most frequent electrolytes. There is a total of approx. 160 grams of salt in the body fluids of humans. Half as much is located in bones, tendons and cartilage. 97% of dissolved sodium chloride is located outside the body cells in the extra cellular space for liquid. The most important task of salt here is to maintain osmotic pressure. The distribution of electrolytes, which is constantly changing, determines the direction of water flow. Our body's water and electrolyte metabolisms are very closely connected. Ion pumps are constantly channelling sodium out of the cells and potassium into them under high energy input.

For optimum functionality of the organism not only the body's own water and the salts dissolved in it have to be at an equilibrium but also the acids and bases. The pH-value of the blood is precisely kept at a constant level, requiring permanent regulation activities during ongoing metabolism. Our body stores sufficient quantities of the minerals sodium, potassium and magnesium in order to neutralise an excess of acids by swiftly producing base forming compounds.

Sodium is involved in the irritability of nerves and muscles and in the activation of enzymes. Chlorine ions enable the high acid concentration in gastric juice, necessary for sound digestion.

A deficiency of common salt may lead to the following disorders:

Nausea, vomiting, spasms, fatigue, reduced elasticity and dehydration of the skin, decrease in blood pressure leading to circulatory collapse (especially with ongoing diarrhoea, vomiting, heavy perspiration, or the application of diuretics), apathy, coma.

An excess intake of table salt may lead to the following disorders:

Fluid retention in the tissue (oedema), hypertension, disorder of nerve and brain functions. The intake of 150 to 200 grams salt can be acutely lethal to humans.

In the course of 14 days, half the sodium chloride within our body is being exchanged. It is excreted through the kidneys, by perspiration and via the intestinal tract.

The relation between common salt in our nutrition and hypertension is today regarded in a less unilateral way today than before. It became known that even with the same level of salt intake people exhibited different levels of blood pressure. There are many people who do not suffer an increase of blood pressure with an increased intake of salt, but in fact their bodies regenerate a balance by increased excretion. In approx. 80% of those suffering from hypertension, the disease is inherited. Only few people actually react sensitively to salt in nutrition. They of course ought to limit their intake of salt. But a sodium-restricted diet is only rarely prescribed these days. The cause for blood pressure in most patients is not due to salt. Furthermore, they show no significant change whether they consume a lot of salt or only very little. It is the sensible changes in our lives that cause the decrease of blood pressure: reduction of weight, physical exercise, giving up smoking, avoiding alcohol. Even relaxation techniques can lead to reduction of blood pressure.

Overall it can be said that today's average nutrition supplies us with more salt than is actually needed. This is mainly because we consume a lot of salt that is "hidden" in meat and sausages, cheese, bread, snacks, sauces, and ready-made food. Fast food and industrially processed food is also heavily salted, simply to make up for the loss of taste. Food in canteens and restaurants is high in salt, too. Chips, seasoned snacks, salt sticks, peanuts, or crisps cannot do without salt, either.

A high salt intake is only problematic when the salt is refined, pure sodium chloride, supplying nothing else but sodium and chloride, lacking any of the collateral minerals and trace elements, which are naturally contained in crystal salt.

If you want to be conscious about what you eat and want to live on a healthy diet you should rather restrict your intake of hidden salts and replace them with natural crystal salt. The greatest effect towards good health can be achieved by completely exchanging the types of salt, not by merely adding crystal salt. The same is true for the drinking of sole (we may also talk of brine) during the so-called "sole cure". From a nutritional point of view there are no reservations against a salt treatment, provided that you abstain from any kind of hidden and refined salt. It does not seem to make sense, however, to consume a fairly small amount of valuable salt on top of all the worthless salt.

Elements of crystal salt

Except for 0.01% to 0.05%, common salt or table salt consists of pure sodium chloride whereas crystalline rock salt is made up of all substances that were dissolved in the primeval sea approx. 250 million years ago. Depending on the source of the salt the content of other natural substances besides sodium chloride varies between 2 and 3%, which means there are 50 to 300 times as many collateral minerals and trace elements contained in it as in evaporated salt. It becomes quite obvious when you look at the coarse chunks of salt from the Himalayas; their reddish tint is due to iron compounds.

Statements are being circulated which list 84 elements apparently present in crystal salt. These statements are, however, not based on chemical analysis but are theoretically derived from the Periodic Table of Elements. The authors of such statements argue that in theory all elements existing on earth – except for the six types of inert gas – must be existent in crystal salt. Whatever scientific chemical-analytical methods for the detection of substances were applied, the majority of elements did not reach the detection limit. Existence of the following elements in crystal salt has been proven: calcium, potassium, magnesium, sulphur oxide, iron, manganese, fluorine, iodine, zinc, chromium, copper, cobalt, and gold. The content of heavy metals is too low to cause any serious concerns from a medical point of view.

Apart from sodium chloride crystalline primeval salt provides essential minerals and trace elements. A few of the most important ones are listed below, along with their most important functions and their deficiency symptoms:

Potassium: pressure inside body cells, activation of enzymes, electrophysiological cell regulation; when deficient: fatigue, nervousness, cardiac rhythm disorders, skin problems, headaches.

Calcium: bone structure, teeth, activation of nerves, muscular contraction, blood coagulation; when deficient: muscle cramps, prickling sensation, numbness, sleep disorders, degeneration of teeth, bleeding.

Magnesium: bone structure, activates more than 300 enzymes, energy metabolism, nerve conduction, hormone production, muscular function, heart; when deficient: muscular weakness, cardiac disorders, bone disorders, nervousness, anxiety, depressions.

Sulphur: present in proteins, activates production of energy, component for bone, cartilage, connective tissue; when deficient: shallow skin colour, dull hair, loose connective tissue, afflicted joints, anxieties.

Silicon: connective tissue, cartilage, bones, teeth, blood vessels, hair, skin; when deficient: skin diseases, accelerated ageing of arteries, loss of hair, brittle nails.

Iron: red blood pigment haemoglobin, oxygen transport, enzymes; when deficient: fatigue, listlessness, anorexia, anaemia, bad skin and hair, lack of concentration.

Zinc: activates many enzymes, part of insulin, protein, carbohydrate and fat metabolism, immune system, growth, detoxification; when deficient: delay of growth, susceptibility to infections, skin alterations, poor wound healing, fatigue, virility dysfunctions, menstruation problems, listlessness, sores at the corners of the mouth, depression.

Manganese: blood coagulation, central nervous system, insulin, thyroid hormones; when deficient: ringing in the ears, hardness of hearing, fatigue, disorders in muscular coordination, afflicted joints, restlessness, pessimism, lack of libido.

Chromium: insulin receptors on body cells, affects level of blood sugar; when deficient: fatigue, irritability, sleep disorders, dizziness, headaches, craving for sweets and alcohol

Copper: haemoglobin synthesis, immune system, bones, pigments in hair and skin; when deficient: faintness, asthenia, decolouration of skin and hair, dermatitis, anaemia.

Cobalt: vitamin B12 component, haemoglobin synthesis, protein structure; when deficient: anaemia with after-effects.

Iodine: thyroid hormones, vitality, coping with stress, energy production, growth; when deficient: struma (goiter), fatigue, excess weight, palpitations, nervousness, inactivity.

Selenium: enzyme component, free radical protection, cell respiration; when deficient: susceptibility to infections, early symptoms of ageing, cardiac diseases.

The relevance of minerals and trace elements is often underestimated although they are of equal importance as vitamins for a healthy function of our entire organism. Sadly, today's nutrition no longer provides a sufficient level of these nutrients and "sparks" to metabolism, because the majority of our food is industrially processed and consists of refined ingredients. Alternative health practitioners therefore increasingly recommend compensating this loss with wholesome crystal salt from the Himalayas. The sole cure has often been a remedy for deficiencies and has achieved amazing subjective and objective improvements of the health status.

More important to us than analysing crystal salt is the knowledge of its integrated wholeness.

For consumption and other purposes it contains sodium chloride at a rate of 98%. While nobody would think of e. g. meeting their demand of iron by consuming crystal salt, the importance of collateral minerals and trace elements must not be impaired just because they only occur in small quantities. Our body only needs traces of them, yet they are indeed needed! If there is a total lack deficiency symptoms occur, just as can be experienced with a lack of vitamins. Equally, an excess intake is also more detrimental than beneficial.

Crystal salt provides a naturally perfect composition of those substances that are dissolved in seawater – a composition that cannot be enhanced by man. Any kind of omission, removal, refinement and manipulation as well as artificial adding can only lead to suboptimal results. Because what could be better than the environmental conditions that led to the onset of existence in the primeval sea? Anything that Life needed was contained therein. Nothing was detrimental, because if it had been, it would not have developed into the abundance of species that we know today and that we humans are part of. Modern insights tell us that it is not only quantity elements that are important for Life, i.e. a healthy, sensible functionality of a living organism. In homeopathy substances are potentised – chemists would call it diluted – in decimal steps of potentiation, eventually rendering the medicine void of any molecules of the original substance. The same is applied for salts: Natrium Chloratum or Natrium Muriaticum are effective although they don't contain the slightest trace of their substance. So why should traces of substances that are contained in primeval salt be of no importance? The entire natural wholeness is always worth more than the combination of all single aspects. Let us not look upon each element individually, but let us make use of the whole, pristine crystal salt!

Why crystal salt from the Himalayas?

The answer is fairly easy: crystalline salt that keeps its natural structure when cleaved from its deposits is of a different quality than refined, pure sodium chloride that is re-crystallised from sole. Apart from different levels of collateral minerals and trace elements, there is another distinction between both types of salt. Crystal salt owns and transports information that is stored in its crystal structure. We know from quartz clocks that crystals can absorb and radiate electro magnetic vibrations. Radioactive atomic waste is stored in abandoned salt mines because radiation is absorbed by salt.

After the sedimentation of sea salt in shallow parts of the primeval sea more than 250 million years ago, the continents began to drift. The salt layer was moved beneath other layers and was subject to immense pressure. Where continents collided mountains folded up. The highest mountains arose in places of highest pressure: the Indian subcontinent drifted against Asia and caused the Himalayas to fold up. They are more than 8,000 metres in height, representing the highest mountains on Earth. It was here that salt sediments suffered utmost pressure, creating salt deposits with large salt crystals. Their structure is sometimes crystal-clear, and they have a reddish-orange tint. We don't know of any other salt that contains more energy than this.

Very sensitive people can feel this energy. Modern tests allow visualisation of it, using the method of pendulum or/and kinesiology. Peter Ferreira carried out biophysical tests by means of segment diagnostics, proving the fact that there are quality distinctions in different types of salt. One may also well know microscopic pictures of spagyric (alchemy) crystallisation: Himalayan salt features fine, lively patterns whereas common table salt and sea salt form strictly rectangular, isolated structures.

The energy contained in Himalayan crystal salt approximates the maximum of measurability. Toxic, i.e. detrimental effects are unknown of. There are, however, certain distinctions, which can probably be accounted for by different deposits or different methods of mining or processing. Rock salt can only consist of those substances that were contained in the respective sea, which dried up. We can assume that each single ocean of the primeval sea had its own specific composition of substances, the variations of which are believed to be similar to that of the salt content of our oceans today. The salt content of the Atlantic Ocean lies at 3.7% while the Black Sea has a salt content of only 1.8%. The Mediterranean Sea contains up to 3.9%, and the Red Sea even as much as 4.0%. The different tints of rock salt are another proof of the different composition of substances in salt, i.e. reddish salt contains a lot more iron than white salt.

In order to retain the positive energy of crystal salt it must not to be mined from its deposits by blasting techniques, nor should it be processed with machines, especially electric ones. The quality of finer types of salt can be preserved by sieving or grinding with stone or ceramic mills. Crystal salt used for cooking should preferably also be ground in a ceramic mill. Just as in homeopathy and other vibration remedies, contact with iron can interfere with its effectiveness. Therefore it is recommended not to use metallic spoons for the measuring of saturated sole!

Critical voices have been asking why qualitative distinctions in salts cannot be measured with "scientific" methods. Some people even go so far as saying that they only accept what science has proven, i.e. if chemical analyses reveal no or only slight differences, then there are none. Therefore, a price difference in salts according to different origins would not be justified. Yet it is worth considering this issue, not just with regard to salt:

From a strictly chemical point of view, a pebble is exactly the same as a rock crystal, just like a piece of coal is the same as a diamond. Not so for experts: To a wine connoisseur there are enormous differences between premium and average wines – reflected in their appreciation and their price. They can be wines of the same variety, or from the same area. Maybe the only difference is actually in the vineyard itself, the producer, or the vintage year. A chemical analysis would reveal no or only insignificant differences. Therefore, an amateur could argue: why should this wine be worth so much more than that wine? The "essential" properties are the same: same level of alcohol, residual sugar,

and acid. The difference can only lie in traces of gustatory substances, occurring only in ever so small quantities. Therefore, they cannot possibly make a difference. The connoisseur argues: it is exactly these differences that cannot be measured and that are only known to the expert which account for the extraordinary value, because these differences come closest to an ideal image, an idea. Nobody would think of questioning the expertise of suppliers and connoisseurs in this "gourmet" area by presenting chemical analyses.

Yet, for crystal salt we do experience this kind of attack with analytical arguments, often on the grounds of economic interests. It is, however, not always possible to capture differences with chemical analyses.

Animals are guided by their instincts. It is a fact that given a choice they strongly prefer organic to conventionally processed food, even though no analytical method can make out a difference between both types. We humans have lost many instincts, or one might also say: we don't trust our "gut" feelings. There are many alternative approaches such as the pendulum or muscle tests, which are particularly suitable to make clear to our inner self how we feel. As to salt: behold the reddish crystals, try their rounded taste and let your emotions decide whether you prefer this or the pure white sodium chloride.

Here is some more guidance for your decision making with regard to quality differences: water can store information. Homeopathic medicine makes use of this feature in potency. The higher the dilution, the higher the value of information. It is presumed that this ability is due to "clusters": water molecules that are in constant movement gather and re-gather to ever-changing patterns, crystal-like structures that vibrate at high frequencies. Water has a "memory". Since we expose it to environmental influences it is negatively charged, but on the other hand it is also positively charged because of certain rock formations that it percolates through, or because of rock crystals and gemstones that help to delete unfavourable frequency patterns and "revive" it, meaning to re-charge it with positive energy.

When salt crystals crystallised from the primeval sea, they stored clusters of the primordial water and reflect them today. Thus it happened that at the onset of evolution 250 million years ago ideal conditions for life were stored and have been preserved over time. Today they yield harmonic vibrations to our body cells as an essence, stimulating our own healing powers.

Here is some more food for thought: Books are all made from paper and ink. That, however, does not mean that chemists can find differences between good and bad literature by carrying out chemical analyses. Does that mean there are no such differences? There are, yet they don't exist on the substantial level, but only on the informational level.

While there is no obligation for anyone to believe in the extraordinary powers of primordial salt, one should at least be unprejudiced and try it on oneself. Replace common table salt with crystal salt, see the effects of a sole cure (exempt from such a cure are kidney patients or people who explicitly suffer from hypertension caused by salt; they should consult their physician first). If you can't feel a difference yourself, ask others for their experiences with crystal salt. You can decide any time you want whether or not some more nature and some wholesomeness are worth a little effort. One thing is for certain: it is not amiss. Quite the contrary: crystal salt has definitely been beneficial to many. Some of the overall benefits and treatments for certain conditions are listed in the next chapter.

Therapeutic benefits of salt

Very basic bodily functions bear on a healthy balance between salts and fluids. This is why salt has been used for thousands of years for the restoration of health. First records of its healing power were reported from ancient Egypt. Healers recommended salt for headaches, skin diseases, dropsy, and gout. The Roman Empire knew that saltwater drinking cures stimulate metabolism and strengthen the immune system.

A description in a health book written by Ibn Botlan (Abu'l Hasan al Muhtar ibn al Hasa ibn Sa'dun) in the 11th century called "Tacuinum Sanitatis", which still exists today in several Arabic and Latin copies, shows how salt was seen as a remedy in Antiquity and into the Middle Ages. Acting on Hippocrate's theory, Ibn Botlan classified all substances into the four categories dry, humid, cold, and warm. Accordingly, salt and seawater is dry and warm whereas fresh water is considered humid and cold. Salt was supposedly good for digestion, prevented decay, but was detrimental to the brain and vision. He recommended salt mainly to the weak, preferably during wintertime and in

Northern regions. Salt water was said to loosen the stomach, salt fish were beneficial to apathetic people.

Since the 19th century, health resorts offering sole baths, sole inhalations, and sole drinking cures have produced increasing interest. The majority of German health resorts are based on therapeutic treatments involving salt, many of which bear related names: Bad Reichenhall, Bad Salzbrunn, Bad Salzschlierf, Bad Salzig, Bad Salzungen, Bad Salzuflen, or Bad Salzdetfurth. They use salt treatments successfully for skin diseases, respiratory conditions, digestive problems, rheumatism, and afflicted joints.

Investigating the healing powers of salts in specific doses was the work of a lifetime for the German physician Dr. Wilhelm Heinrich Schuessler (1821 to 1898). His healing principle is based on the fact that only 12 mineral salts remain after the cremation of a corpse; all other organic components such as fat, proteins, or sugar will be entirely destroyed during the process. Health, according to his definition, is the balance between these 12 salts. His "biochemical healing principle" aims at balancing deficits, or unhealthy distributions, by adding mineral salts. Not in their pure substances though, but in potentised form according to homeopathic methods.

Schuessler developed twelve „biochemical functional remedies" by putting one part salt to nine parts lactose and grinding them thoroughly. The result was the first decimal potency (D1). For further potentiation this potency is again "diluted" in the same way. Common salt is known as Natrium Chloratum or Natrium Muriaticum and is functional remedy no. 8. In homeopathy it is used for the following conditions:

Emaciation, anorexia, listlessness, anaemia, chlorosis, headaches, migraine, watery gastrointestinal catarrh.

Natrium Chloratum ointment is applied externally for acne, herpes, skin fungus and insect bites.

It comes as no surprise that the principle of Schuessler's salt treatments matches that of homeopathic treatments and even corresponds to recommendations dating back to Antiquity.

Salt (yan) in Chinese dietetics is classified as being cold with regard to temperature characteristics. Its effect is described as detoxifying, having a harmonising effect on the "centre" and decreasing the "Qi". It is proven that it was applied as early as the 3rd century B. C. for sensation of fullness, obstipation, sore throats, toothache, and gum bleeding.

Common salt has proven to be very beneficial for pain treatment. The German practitioner Dr. Volker Desnizza found out that the injection of isotonic saline solution yields considerable success with backache, herniated discs, rheumatism and migraine. The sodium iones contained in salt activate the nerves concerned, initiating the body's own healing process.

External application of salt

Sole bath

Although the external application of salt has been a well-known fact since Antiquity, the use of sole (or brine) only started to increase during the 18th century when seaside health resorts boomed. Christoph Wilhelm Hufeland, physician of Germany's most famous poets Schiller and Goethe, wrote a book about the external application of salt and so promoted this development further. Consequently, places with sole springs or salt deposits turned into spas.

The concentration of salt in a sole bath lies between 1 and 8 percent. Because of favourable results that were achieved with highly concentrated, natural sole from the Dead Sea, even higher concentrations of 12% and more are used for the treatment of psoriasis.

Depending on the composition and the concentration level of salts, sole baths may affect the circulatory system and should not be taken unassisted. To begin with, the bath should take no longer than 5 to 10 minutes and can afterwards be extended to a maximum of 20 minutes. The water temperature must not exceed 38°C. It is recommended to take no more than two baths a week when applying the treatment at home. The skin must be dabbed dry after the bath and the patient is required to stay in bed for one hour. Only afterwards should the salt be washed off and cream be applied to the skin.

It is best to use crystal bath salt from the Himalayas for sole baths and all other forms of external application. Under no circumstances can salts with chemical or artificial additives be used. For one full bath of 120 litres, 1.2 kg of salt are required to make a 1% saline solution. Let the appropriate quantity dissolve entirely in a little lukewarm water. Then fill up the bath. Take care not to exceed the temperature of 38°C. When dissolving, salt causes the water to cool down. So if you were to run your bath first and then add the salt it would cool down the temperature of your water.

The main application of sole baths is for the treatment of skin irritations such as psoriasis and neurodermatitis, as well as rheumatism and joint problems outside acute attacks. Their effects are not limited to the skin but indeed go much deeper: they act on the nervous system and on the regulation of inflammation processes: sole baths are relaxing, refreshing, they cheer you up and give new energy. They activate generation of glucocorticoid in the adrenal cortex and help to suppress any inflammations.

The immediate effect on the skin is the deposit of salt water in the external corneal layer whereas pure fresh water causes the water-fat-protective-layer to macerate, even removes it, prompting more fluids in the skin to evaporate. The skin becomes dry and requires the application of cream for its restoration. Sole baths have a less drying effect and are always suitable when dry and rough skin is concerned.

Sole baths are effective for arthrosis, chronic poly arthritis, gout, muscle tension, psycho vegetative exhaustion, menopause and menstruation problems, skin irritations, blood circulation disorders, neurodermatitis, psoriasis, vein conditions and an insufficient immune system. The extensive contact with salt water at body temperature reminds us of our pre-natal condition in the amniotic sac, which prompts our body to re-tune and activate its own healing powers.

Sole washings

For nose, throat and eyes washing, a 0.9% iso-tonic saline solution is used. Dissolve 9 grams of salt in 1 litre of lukewarm water. Gargling with salt water moistens the inflamed mucous membrane, removing bacteria and scaled cells – a blessing for sore throats!

Nasal douches or nasal cleansing pots are available for nose washings. The nose cone is inserted into one nostril, keeping it fully sealed. The pot is lifted and the head is slightly tilted sideways so that the water can flow out of the other nostril. Note that one must breathe through the mouth while water is flowing through and that the wastewater ought to be directed into the sink. The procedure is repeated with the other nostril. In case of a cold, the salt content can be slightly increased in order to prompt the nose to run. Mucus can drain off, even from sinuses. For obvious reasons guarding one self against diseases is always better than healing them. Many people swear by daily nasal washings as a prophylaxis to colds. People suffering from hay fever and headaches find great relief in nasal douches.

Eye washings are carried out with an eye cup – a small glass or plastic vessel (available in drug stores). Remove all make-up first, fill the vessel with sole, hold the cup to your eye, tip your head back and open and close your eye to allow the solution to wet the eye.

Sole ointments, compresses and packs

For open wounds only isotonic saline solution can be used. For skin irritations the concentration level can lie at up to 8%, the same level as in a sole bath. Even insect bites, sprained joints, bruises, and swellings can be treated with saturated sole.

For compresses, a clean cotton or linen cloth is immersed in sole and applied to the affected area. Cold sole compresses have been helpful in bruises, sprained joints, inflamed tendon sheaths and as leg compresses to reduce body heat. Warm compresses alleviate rheumatic and joint problems.

A very special variation are salt socks: cotton socks are soaked in 3% sole solution, wrung dry and put on. Another pair of dry wool socks is put on top. Leave for one hour. Salt socks improve the condition of blood circulation, chronic cold feet, and gout.

The salt shirt works according to the same principle and is regarded as an enhancement of the "full body wrap" by Kneipp. The shirt has to stick closely to the body after it has been wrung dry. When staying in bed during treatment, the salt shirt may lead to hyperthermia; it should not be applied for more than one hour, and not without assistance. The salt shirt promotes metabolism and detoxification. A prolonged rest or some sleep after treatment is recommended.

Inhalation of sole

The seaside is an ideal place for natural sole inhalation. In the surf zone the salt content in the air is even measurable. The same is true for the immediate vicinity of grading works in sole spa resorts. Large constructions covered with black thorn give off a gentle spray of sole (brine), which is caught and spread by the wind, dispensing salt into the air. Inhalations are essential ways of treating respiratory diseases such as bronchitis, chronic sinusitis, and asthma.

At home you can do sole inhalation by yourself. Pour 1 – 2 litres of water into a large pot and add crystalline primeval salt. Heat it up until steam begins to rise. Cover up your head with a big towel, keep your head above the pot for approx. 15 minutes and inhale the sole steam.

To begin with, the sole concentration level should slightly exceed 0.9% because then the steam extracts water from the mucous membrane and acts as an expectorant. The concentration level can be increased to 3% because a higher concentration is more effective mainly in the lower air passages.

For inhalations prescribed by health practitioners there are a number of spray nozzles or ultra sound nebulisers available, allowing the size of water drops to be adjusted. Such nebulisers as are used in room fountains ought not to be operated with sole since the size of water drops cannot be regulated, making them unfit for medical treatment. If you want to enhance your room air with sole, you ought to refrain from using this kind of nebuliser because their sole spray would be far too aggressive for your room furnishings! Best results are achieved with a zeolite-salt water fountain. Zeolite is a natural crystal made from alkali silicate or earthy base aluminium silicate. It is found in basalt crevices and cavities. Its loosely-bound structure is highly porous and pervaded by microscopic canals. Zeolite consists of silicon, aluminium, oxygen, potassium and sodium. It is ideal for ion exchange, and acts as a filter and catalyst. Zeolite is used as a natural filter in e.g. ponds, aquariums, and for water preparation. When sole trickles across zeolite we can experience the same effect as with grading works: fine salt as well as negatively charged ions (as with crystal salt lamps) are dispensed into the air. Smoke, dust and other kinds of pollution are filtered from the air, giving the room a mild stimulating sea-like climate. It gives relief to all those who suffer from respiratory problems.

Internal application of salt:
Sole drinking cure

Sole drinking cures rank among the oldest salt treatments. Even the Roman physician Galen already prescribed them. In Medieval days detailed descriptions for the application of drinking cures were available, explaining the use of increasing and decreasing levels of saline concentration to promote urination and diarrhoea. Seawater drinking cures became fashionable, too. To this day, some seaside health resorts still offer bottled seawater for drinking cures. But in general it is water from natural sole springs, also called spa water, with a therapeutically relevant mineral content of more than 1 gram of salt per litre that is used today. Depending on its source it contains other minerals among sodium such as calcium, magnesium, potassium, chlorine, sulphate and hydrogen carbonate as well as trace elements such as iron, iodine, or fluoride. They are in general the same substances as can be found in Himalayan crystal salt. It must be said, though, that these minerals occur in different combinations, according to their source.

Drinking cures with these highly concentrated spa waters are generally prescribed for gastric and intestinal problems, gall and liver conditions, inflamed urinary tracts, gout, diabetes, osteoporosis, exhaustion, and allergies.

A sole drinking cure involving Himalayan crystal salt is different from a spa water drinking cure in such a way that it is no treatment of an existing illness but rather a prophylaxis for the promotion of good health, or maybe an accompaniment to other treatments. It does not require medical prescription. You can apply it at home unassisted. Strictly speaking, the term "cure" is not altogether true because cures are always limited as to time whereas sole made of Himalayan crystal salt can be taken without any time limit. Compared to spa water cures, this sole cure supplies our human body with less mineral salts, i.e. approx. 1 – 2 grams of salt, which can easily be saved on other parts of our diet. The sole drinking cure is not about the quantity of salt but about its quality and the information delivered with it. The less refined salt is consumed with overall nutrition, the better Himalayan crystal salt can act. Therefore, make sure to use Himalayan crystal salt for cooking, freshly ground with a ceramic salt mill, or use the saturated sole for the seasoning of your food. Reduce your consumption of convenience food when you are uncertain which kind of salt was used in the preparation of it.

The effects of a sole drinking cure are drastic and clearly noticeable. Connective tissue is detoxified, contaminations are washed out. The body is retuned, energy blockades are lifted and the body's own healing powers are stimulated. Initial aggravation may occur, even a health crisis accompanied by diarrhoea, headaches, fatigue, or nausea. These are no drawbacks but a positive sign for the ongoing healing process.

The sole drinking cure gives you new energy and new strength. The balance of minerals and trace elements is restored and partly accounts for the new well-being. Your body cells experience an impulse because they have contact with the ideal environment from the primeval sea where all life originates. Metabolism is stimulated, and a healthy balance develops.

The more you are removed from a natural way of living, the longer it takes for the sole drinking cure to become effective. Those who consume wholesome food, don't smoke, don't drink alcohol, and don't take any chemical drugs, those whose organism is experienced in gentle vibration treatments such as homeopathy, Bach Flowers, or kinesiology will not have to wait long to experience the pleasant effects of the sole drinking cure.

The sole drinking cure is suitable for everyone. Exempt from this therapy are only those who suffer from grave insufficiency of the kidneys, the cardiovascular system, or from hypertension due to responsiveness to common salt. The cure alone may not always be the long hoped for panacea, depending on the person's predisposition and earlier therapies. Yet it supports anybody who wants to maintain good health and keep in shape, or wants to return to this state by using natural resources.

How to prepare your sole drink:

You start by making a saturated sole from a few rocks of Himalayan crystal salt. Often, rocks or granulate are already offered in glass jars for this purpose. Otherwise you place the rocks or granulate into a glass jar. Cover them with water and let them stand for approx. 8 hours. The sole is saturated when no more crystals dissolve. It has a salt concentration of approx. 26%. When the sole runs low add fresh water. The sole will remain saturated for as long as rocks are still visible. It is sterile. Germs stand no chance in this salt concentration. It will keep forever.

How to administer the sole drinking cure:

Every morning, take a drop of the saturated sole, increasing the quantity to one teaspoon (plastic – no metal spoon!), put it into a glass and fill up with water. It is best to take this glass in the morning before breakfast. It does not taste very salty and is not as unpleasant as you may think. You may also drink the sole throughout the day by putting a teaspoon of sole into a bottle of water.

Children only need a few drops of sole. In case of strong reactions, especially in the shape of cleansing of the bowels, reduce the quantity to just a few drops, and increase again when you see that you show a better tolerance.

An important note on water

During the process of preparing sole, the primeval salt that was stored in a dry place for 250 million years comes into contact again with the medium from which it had crystallised before. Information from the salt is received by water and passed on to us. It is obvious that no tap water can be used for this purpose since it is charged with negative information and substances, because of its origin and it has been treated in water works. The ideal water for the preparation of sole and for dilution should contain as few mineral substances as possible. Most suitable is water that was cleansed by way of reverse osmosis and energised with gemstones. Ideal is pure, non-carbonated spring water, which has the same energy level as Himalayan salt. Look out for still waters with low mineral content, energised through natural rock formations. It should not be carbonated but should have been bottled without the use of pressure.

Salt for beauty

The skin is the largest organ of human bodies. Skin irritations are always related to intestinal and/ or psychic problems in one way or the other. Our skin is – as the saying goes – the mirror of our soul. Eczema, neurodermatitis and psoriasis are only the most extreme, visible signs of something else that is wrong deep down inside of us. If e.g. the healthy intestinal balance is in disorder, the skin must take over certain excretion functions, resulting in skin impurities or acne.

From time immemorial, salt has been applied externally. A sole bath is a blessing for stressed, dry and irritated skin. Skin dander is cast-off, stimulating new production. The application of sole is helpful with inflammations. It combats germs and pyogenic bacteria.

Sole sludge is indicated for masks and facial packs. A sole sludge facial pack restores moisture, regenerates and tightens your skin. Sole sludge is especially effective for cellulite.

Should you not be able to obtain sole sludge you can mix healing earth with finely ground Himalayan crystal salt 1:1 and add some water. Let it work for approx. 15 minutes.

For thousands of years, salt has been used for dental hygiene. Chinese medical science recommends the chewing of coarsely ground salt in the morning to guard oneself against periodontosis and gum bleeding. My tip for you: rinse your mouth in the mornings and evenings with saturated sole made from Himalayan crystal salt (sole toothpaste is available, too!). Take 1 – 2 minutes to gargle and rinse water through your teeth.

Salt crystal lamps

The soothing effect of salt crystal lamps can be used to enhance the room climate considerably. We spend a lot of time indoors where the air is charged with dust, tobacco smoke, gases of synthetic materials in furniture, electrical appliances, and fabrics. The distribution of ions in the room air is another factor for subjective well-being. Ions are atoms that have either too many or too few electrons; due to their imbalanced electrical charge ratio they are either negative (minus-ion), or positive (plus-ion).

Minus-ions have a healing effect on us humans. We feel best where the air is charged with a majority of minus-ions: at the sea, near waterfalls, after a rainfall in the forest, or in the mountains. Usually, plus-ions predominate indoors because of central heating, electronic devices, television, computers, and smoking.

When crystal salt is warmed up, it emits more minus-ions. A salt crystal lamp can be created by placing an electric bulb inside a large rock of crystal salt. This will enrich the surrounding air with negative ions, and thus improve the room climate, creating a seaside atmosphere. The red tone of the light that is being radiated has a calming and warming effect, is strengthening, uplifting, and supports the immune system. Ask specifically for salt crystal lamps from the Himalayan region because they ideally underline the effects of the sole drinking cure.

Salt in whole food cooking

We have almost come to the end of this little booklet, and yet not much has been said so far about the use of salt in our kitchen. Of course it would be of no use to apply the sole drinking cure on the one hand, and on the other continue to use the "empty" table salt with its free-flowing agents. It ought to be replaced with crystal salt granulate which is ground in a salt mill. Never use a metallic grinding mechanism but rather one made from ceramic. Finely ground crystal salt from the Himalayas should not have any free-flowing agents added to it. The slight disadvantage of this is that the air humidity makes the salt clump together. It can be loosened by tapping against the jar. However, the problem can be avoided entirely by using a salt mill.

In former times, salt was used in large quantities for the preparation of food. Bread was baked, meat and fish pickled, and vegetable was preserved in sole solutions; there is no production of cheese without salt. Today, these production processes have largely been taken over by respective industries, and we go and buy ready-made products. The more ready-made food is used in a kitchen, the less salt is needed. But those who make a point of preparing their own food themselves by using raw, freshly harvested vegetables, cereals, etc. use more salt and have a good opportunity of replacing less valuable salt with crystal salt from the Himalayas. Therefore, I appeal to you: be your own cook, because only then do you have a choice of what you eat. Use crystal salt with a clear conscience because you now know about its potential. Don't restrict yourself to salt alone. Make use of the abundance of spices and herbs to refine your dishes!

Books

Salz, Macht, Geschichte. (Salt, Power, History.) Bayerische Staatskanzlei 1995

Schweiger, Anita, *Heilen mit Salz. (Healing with Salt.)* München 2000

Hendel, Barbara, Ferreira, Peter, *Wasser & Salz. (Water and Salt.)* Herrsching 2001

F. Batmanghelidj, M.D. *Your Body's Many Cries For Water.* 1997

Kaussner, Erwin, *Kristallines Salz – Elixier der Jugend (Crystalline Salt – Elixier of Youth.)* Siegsdorf 2001

Desnizza, Volker, *Schmerzfrei durch Kochsalz (Free of Pain through Table Salt.)* Köln 1996

Dr. Joel D. Wallach & Dr. Ma Lan, *Dead Doctors Don't Lie.* 1999, 2004

Weihofen, Jürgen, *Heilpilze Ling Zhi, Shiitake & Co. schützen das Immunsystem. (Healing Mushrooms Ling Zhi, Shiitake etc. Protect the Immune System.)* Troisdorf 2000

Weihofen, Jürgen, *Aloe Vera – die Heilkraft der Wüstenpflanze für Gesundheit und Schönheit. (Aloe*

Vera – the Healing Powers of a Desert Plant for Health and Beauty.) Troisdorf 2003

Weihofen, Jürgen, *Noni – die Zauberfrucht aus der Südsee für Gesundheit und Lebensqualität. (Noni – a Magical Fruit from the South Seas to provide Health and Quality of Life.)* Troisdorf 2004

Sources

Crystal salt from the Himalayas can be obtained from health food shops, natural food shops, shops for esotericism, and mail order catalogues. Available are washed and cleansed rocks for nutrition purposes (approx. 2 – 3 cm in diameter), granulate for salt mills, and fine salt.

Heartfelt Living Health Products Inc.
Sole Importer & Distributor
Phone : (604) 898-SALT toll free: 1-888-898-SALT
www.heartfeltliving.com info@heartfeltliving.com
- *High Quality Himalayan Crystal Salt, Salt Grinder*
- *Bath Salts, Mask, Cosmetics, Shampoo*
- *Crystal Salt Lamps & Tea Lights and much more...*

Circle of Health – Joanne Garrison, Owner
6150 Valley Way # 202, Niagara Falls, ON
L2E 1Y3 – Canada Phone: (905) 371-3331
www.circleofhealth.ca circleofhealth@bellnet.ca
- *Offering Electro Dermal Testing for Organ Evalutions & Allergy Testing*
- *Reflexology & Indian Head Massage.*

Florence's Health Connection
PO Box 1624, St. Paul, AB, T0A 3A0 – Canada
Phone: 1-780-645-2160   Fax: 1-780-645-3077
e-mail: flolab@telus.net
- *Himalayan Crystal Salt Products*
- *Bio Pro Cell & Fuel Chips*
- *Enrich Herbal Products.*

ILLUMINATIONS STATION
130 8th Avenue S., Safety Harbor, FL, 34695 – USA
Phone: 1-727-797-4441   Fax: 1-727-797-4445
www.illuminationsstation.com
A Holistic, Spiritual Store selling Massage Supplies, Unique Gifts, which houses Crystal's Cave with 200 lighted Salt Rock Lamps and Himalayan Crystal Salt.

For Information on Himalayan Crystal Salt in Winnipeg, MB, Canada
- Please call Cathryn Nykvist @ 1-204-885-0723
- Aromatherapist, Herbalist
- Doula & Pranic Healer.

PreZENse of Mind – Contact Kelly Baird
Experience the Power of Peace with Meditation
Bring Balance & Harmony to Body, Mind & Spirit
with the Ancient Healing Arts – Reiki, Reflexology,
Hot Stone Massage, Ear Candling & More.
Ph: (780) 418-0686 Toll Free: (877) 557-0240
prezense@shaw.ca   www.prezenseofmind.com

THE HOBBIT HOUSE – Leanne Kunka RA, Owner
71 South 1st Avenue, Williams Lake, BC
V2G 1H7 – Canada   e-mail: severson@wlake.com
Phone: 1-250-392-7599 Fax: 1-250-392-7590
*Wholistic Wellness Center – Therapy, Wellness
Products, Metaphysical Wares*

Triangle Healing Products – Diane Regan, Owner
772 Spruce Avenue, Victoria, BC, V8T 5A5 Canada
Phone: 1-250-370-1818   toll free: 1-888-370-1818
trianglehealingproducts.comtrianglehealing@shaw.ca
*Air Purifiers, Shields, Chi Machines, Distillers,
Emethy, Far-Infrared Saunas, Juicers, Medical
Magnets, Platinum Energy Foot Spas and more.*

WHOLISTIC HEALTH, Marianne Goetsch RT-CRA
Reiki Teacher/Practitioner, Foot Reflexologist, EFT,
CCMBA & CCSMS, Meditation Instructor. Member
of: AMTWP, CRA and Touchpoint Reflexology &
Kinesthetics. Reiki Workshops for Kids age 4-12.
12221-54 St. Edmonton, AB. T5W 3N6
Phone: (780) 479-0620 e-mail: ewg@telusplanet.net

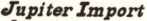

FACE ESSENTIALS

Highest Quality Essential Oil Blend for Beautiful & Healthy Skin
Formulated & distributed by:
Renata Hussinger
Aromatherapist

Escape the dangers of mainstream skin care products and choose this safe
and effective therapeutic-grade essential oil blend as an
Alternative to a Skin Cream.

Two blends are available for:

All Skin Types
Hypersensitive Skin and Broken Capillaries
also excellent for dry skin

FACE ESSENTIALS was specifically formulated for the facial
skin and throat, is not greasy and does not clog pores.
The components of both blends were carefully chosen to:

- combat premature aging of the skin
- purify the skin and underlaying tissues
- restores the skin's elasticity and to firm and tone
- combat sagging skin
- prevent oxidative damage
- rejuvenate and heal damaged skin while preventing and retarding wrinkles
- help with acne, dermatitis, eczema & detoxification

Experience a youthful, radiant & healthy look, reduced lines,
more refined and tighter skin and lessened age spots.

For complete information and ingredients list, please visit our website:
www.the-body-clinic.ca
Ask for these products at your Health Food Store or order from:

THE BODY CLINIC
Lakeview Mall
Burns Lake, B.C. Canada
Phone/Fax: 1-250-692-7755
www.the-body-clinic.ca
E-mail: sales@the-body-clinic.ca